MW00895264

THE NEW SHOE

JEFF MacNELLY

AVON
PUBLISHERS OF BARD, CAMELOT, DISCUS AND FLARE BOOKS

To Mom

THE NEW SHOE is an original publication of Avon Books. This work
has never before appeared in book form.

AVON BOOKS
A division of
The Hearst Corporation
959 Eighth Avenue
New York, New York 10019
Copyright © 1981 by Jefferson Communications, Inc.
Published by arrangement with Jefferson Communications, Inc.
Library of Congress Catalog Card Number: 81-65074
ISBN: 0-380-78030-5

For further information address Jefferson Communications,
11730 Bowman Green Drive, Reston, Virginia 22090

First Avon Printing, September, 1981

AVON TRADEMARK REG. U.S. PAT. OFF. AND IN OTHER COUN-
TRIES, MARCA REGISTRADA, HECHO EN U.S.A.

Printed in the U.S.A.

10 9 8 7 6 5 4 3 2 1

Front Section

3

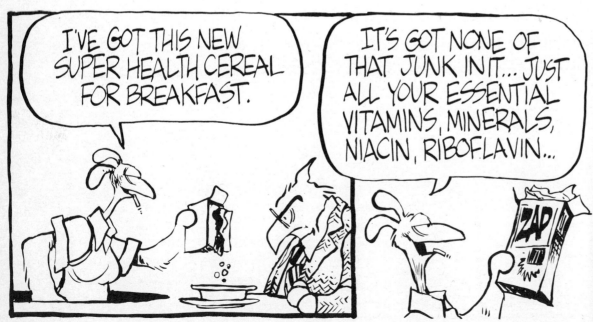

Dear Perfesser,
I'm a college freshman and I want to be a columnist.

I'm bright and I am an excellent writer, perceptive with an engaging wit. But what courses should I take?

Start with Humility 101.

Dear Perfesser,
I'm a freshmen at Literati A and M, and I want to be a investagative reportor.

What should I major in?

Spelling.

Dear Perfesser,
With food prices going sky high, and no end in sight

Where can I put my money so I can be sure of staying ahead of inflation?

Invest in long-term hamburger.

Dear Perfesser:
What should you look for on a wine label when shopping?

I don't know about you,

but I look for "#1.69."

Good wine should be served in the proper container.

Some wines are presented nicely in elegant decanters...

some, in sensible carafes for the table.

Others are served in more informal containers.

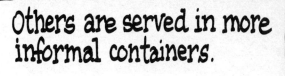

Dear Perfesser:
I'm serving Mexican pizza, chili with garlic and anchovies, and red onion salad....

What kind of wine would go best with this feast?

May I suggest a Chateau Listerino...

11

15

Ask the Perfesser

Dear Perfesser,
My boyfriend and I are having problems. He *hates* John Travolta, and refuses to go to the disco with me when I wear my tinfoil halter dress.

And he hates my favorite drink — muscatel and root beer.
Do you think our relationship can work?

Nope.
He's too good for you.

Dear Perfesser,
I have some money to invest, but I don't want to put it in the stock market. I have heard there are some interesting opportunities in livestock. True?

Yes, indeed.

TAP TAP

In fact, I just heard about a sure thing in the third race today at Dogfood Downs...

TAP TAP

Dear Editor,
    Your crummy paper's stories are all slanted and inaccurate. Your editorials are ridiculous clap trap. And you run the silliest paper in the world.

Furthermore, I am sure you won't print this letter.
    — Genghis Boomer

Dear Mr. Boomer:
    All of your statements are completely wrong — except the last one...

TAPPA TAP

MACNELLY 6/15

Perfesser's DO-IT-YOURSELF column:

Dear Perfesser:
    You once wrote a great column on tool sheds. I don't know the date, but it was sometime after World War II. Could you look it up for me?

Do it yourself.

TAPPA TIP

MACNELLY 7/26

22

Perfesser's <u>Do-It-Yourself</u> Hints:
How to convert your single bed into a spacious king-size.

First of all...

it helps if you're 2 feet 3.

OKAY, SKYLER... TEN MORE SIT-UPS AND WE'RE THROUGH.

YOU DO NINE, AND I'LL DO ONE.

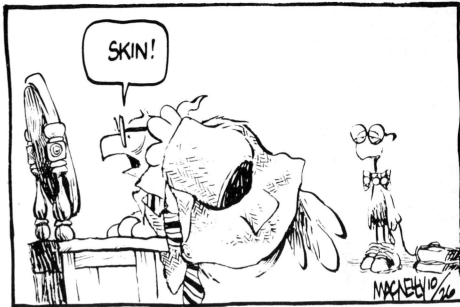

Section II

GEEZ, ANOTHER TALK SHOW...

HI! WE'RE TALKING WITH FEMINIST GLORIA STERNUM.

AND, HEY, GLORIA, THE WOMEN'S MOVEMENT HAS REALLY MADE SOME PROGRESS, HASN'T IT?

IT SURE HAS, MERV...

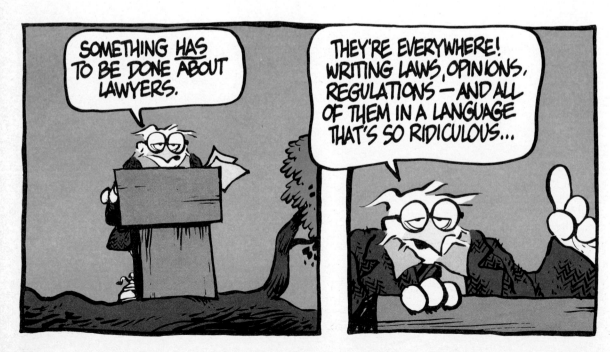

Ask the Perfesser.

Dear Perfesser,

My boyfriend is handsome, brilliant, and very rich.

He is always buying me flowers and gives me expensive presents just for the fun of it.

He's a neat person and we have a lot of fun together. He is very fond of me and I think he is the greatest!

The trouble is, he says we shouldn't get too serious about each other just yet.

Should I ditch him and find a guy who wants to get serious with me?

MACNELLY 11/12

Get serious.

44

45

WHAT THE HECK IS THIS?

HEY, SHOE, I DON'T KNOW ABOUT THIS NEW FEATURE WE'RE RUNNING.

WHAT'S WRONG WITH IT?

WELL, IT'S JUST NOT WHAT YOU'D EXPECT TO SEE IN A DIGNIFIED NEWSPAPER...

51

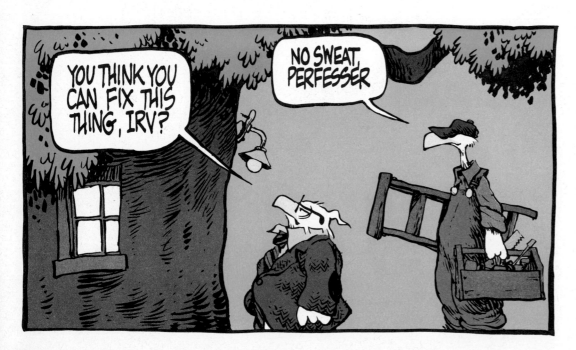

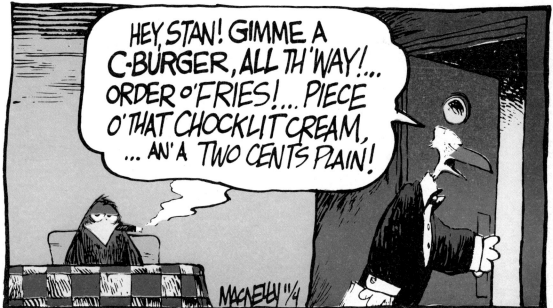

(otherwise known by his nom de plume, or pen-name, Mark Twain) is a very hard and difficult job indeed and requires a lot of careful study.

The first thing that one must do when one is asked to compare the theme of Tom Sawyer to the theme of Treasure Island is to find out where the two books are the same, if they are.

But also, however, be that as it may, the fact remains that while we want to find the points where the two books are the same when we compare the two themes, we want to also find out, if we can, where the two books are different if indeed they are different at all.

In fact, such a question as comparing the themes of Treasure Island and Tom Sawyer is so difficult and complex a question that it certainly can't be properly discussed in a book report of only two hundred words of which this is the two-hundredth.

MACNELLY 1/6

81

THE ONLY POLL THAT COUNTS IS ON ELECTION DAY, Y'KNOW...

ANYWAY, I'VE ALREADY TAKEN STEPS TO CORRECT THESE POLL RESULTS.

I TALKED TO MY PERSONAL POLLSTER JUST THIS MORNING...

AND **FIRED** THE LYIN' SNAKE!

MACNELLY 3/16

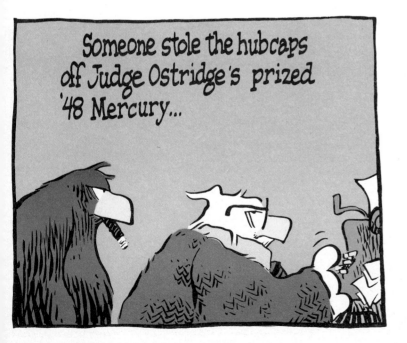

91

Section C

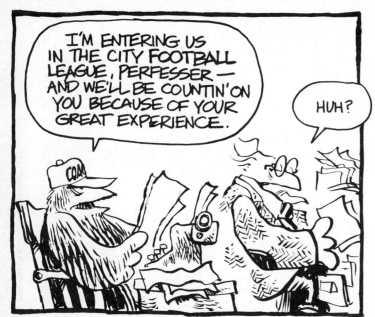

WE'LL RUN THE GREEN 42, ZIG OUT, CIRCLE FIVE... SPLIT YELLOW...ON TWO!

LET'S GO!

HUT! HUT!

THE ORIGINAL ARMCHAIR QUARTERBACK.

MACNELLY 10/13

GEEZ! 115 CARDS HERE, AND NOT ONE REAL SUPERSTAR

WELL, COLLECTING BASEBALL CARDS IS A LOT LIKE LIFE, SKYLER...

FOR EVERY TOM SEAVER, THERE ARE 28 IRWIN BLIDGETTES.

MACNELLY

103

1. What was the Peloponnesian War?

It was a war in Peloponnesia.

THAT SHOULD BE GOOD FOR HALF A POINT, AT LEAST.

Define the following:

Spruce

A dapper pine tree.

Geography test:
Identify the following:

Crimea.

River made famous in song by Julie London.

MACNELLY 12/1

Identify the following:
1. Sir Walter Raleigh.

1. He was a famous Englishman

who discovered the capital of North Carolina.

MACNELLY 12/10

Dear Subscriber:
Your subscription to Procrastination Review is about to expire.

To renew, simply mail us the enclosed card after checking the appropriate box below:

Bill me later............☐
Bill me much later...☐

LET'S SEE HERE...
THE BANK SAYS I HAVE $28.72 IN MY CHECKING ACCOUNT.

AND ACCORDING TO MY CALCULATIONS, I'M $1264.44 OVERDRAWN.

CLOSE ENOUGH.

Dear Mr. Fishhawk:
Your check to us for $52.95 has been returned by your bank marked "insufficient funds."

We will be unable to start your correspondence course until proper payment has been made..

Yours truly,
the *Famous Accountants' School*

Longtime racing fan "Longshot Larry" Furlong died yesterday at age 92.

Furlong was a fixture at the Goose Bump Downs Raceway.

OBITUARIES

In lieu of flowers, the family asks that contributions be put on "Flatfoot Freddy" in the third race this Saturday...

MACNELLY 10/18

THAT SUGGESTION BOX IS REALLY CRAMMED.

I'D BETTER TAKE CARE OF THAT...

SUGGESTIONS

FLOOMP!

MACNELLY 5/22

111

113

Dear grandma:
I hope you had a nice Christmas.

Thank you for the Lawrence Welk sweat shirt...

SHEEZ!

It's the cat's pajamas.

LAWREN

GREAT... MY SHIRTS ARE BACK FROM THE CLEANERS...

AND THERE'S NOTHING BETTER THAN SLIDING INTO A FRESH, CLEAN SH... OH NO!...

STARCH.

117